The Place I'm Going

Lucy Alice Dickens

BookLeaf Publishing
India | USA | UK

The Place I'm Going © 2021

Lucy Dickens

All rights reserved.

No part of this publication may be reproduced, stored in a retrieval system, or transmitted, in any form or by any means, electronic, mechanical, photocopying, recording or otherwise, without the prior written permission of the presenters.

Lucy Dickens asserts the moral right to be identified as the author of this work.

Presentation by *BookLeaf Publishing*

Web: www.bookleafpub.com

E-mail: info@bookleafpub.com

ISBN: 9789357447065

First edition 2021

This poetry book is dedicated to my husband who has been a great support for me over the past decade in pursuing college, a military career, and now my writing. He knows to be patient when I have a poem flowing through my veins and to provide me with inspiration when I don't have the creative juices flowing. Love you babe.

PREFACE

Long ago I wrote a poem about an expectation that I would one day be in a "single point in space and time where my whole world converges." A few years later, I found myself a patient in a military hospital struggling with intense pain. However, I almost immediately recognized my two week duration in that ward as that point that connected my experiences from the past with my trajectory for the future. I will never say that pain or bad things happen for a reason. However, I will say being a poet made it easier for me to find symbolism within that experience.

Meet This Moment

Can you meet this moment
Does inspiration come?
Or do you sit this second
Just twiddling your thumbs

Do you sit idly by
As the world passes in state
To only watch and criticize,
To the crumbling crowd berate?

Or are you lying broken
Afraid to act again
Waiting for some token
To leave your dragon's den

Is your hoard gathering
With things that once had use
But now sit dust collecting
No gold chunks left to sluice

You can meet this moment
Please say these words with me
I believe we will summit
This pass to become free

Observation

More than life is put on hold
More than fungus onto mold
All is but disintegration
All that falls from segregation

Deep down dark
Escapes a lark
What is worn
Cannot be torn

What a creeping queer sensation
Breaking every known convention
Approaching now the dreary end
Of where that flat map starts to bend

Dreams, oh dreams
Of what is gone
Up the stream
To where we spawn

Money

Curse you.
I hate you.
I loathe that I have to spend
Every free moment
Counting what I can send.

Somedays
I find ways
To circumvent those needs
Searching what I can make
From small discarded seeds

Other times
I relish limes
And drinks I get from you
Then hate myself for enjoying
The things you let me do

My family
Was sensibly
Inclined to win your favor
It worked out well for them
But now I taste a different flavor

Could I rely
Just scraping by
Without losing a penny?

But no, my hoard will never grow
Do I need money? Any.

Doomsday Prepping

In 2012 they told us
The world was going to end
We laughed at it in public
But in private, our worries we'd tend

In 2016 they told us
A women would be president
Then watched so many crumble
At the promise that wasn't sent

Then 2020 showed us
A doomsday every day
The four horsemen gathered
But we somehow found a way

What will four years bring us?
What have four years taught?
Are we stronger because of this,
Or lamenting the damages wrought?

When I saw doomsday preppers
From eras of before
I point out flaws in logic
That I now can not ignore.

I know to live on canned goods
Can only last so long.
I'd rather establish garden woods
To make my veggies strong.

I also know that firearms,
Though useful in a fight
Also inspire alarms
To the coming doom fright

In 2024, they tell us
Prepare for global weirding.
Evacuate plans and neighborhood skills
Are the newest doomsday prepping.

Slaughter Me

You have slaughtered me
And I cannot recover
I have not the wits
To redress my rebuttal
Days turn into weeks
Weeks turn into years
Someday you will regret my death
And drown in your own tears
You have slaughtered me, my friend
But that will cause your cancer
The shadow hanging over you
Will your crimes soon answer.

Lamb

When did I become a lamb?
What age did I stop
Gently bleating to the wolf
Each time I was caught?

Where did I pick up the guts
To fight back after folding
How did I learn to fire the guns
I didn't know I was holding?

Who manifested this change in me
Which predator can I blame?
Why did I recreate myself
With such bitter disdain?

I am the one who changed myself.
It was my words that tainted
Transforming from a gentle elf
Into a dark drow instead

But I have faith
For I have seen
The truth of reincarnation
I will bleat and return to the fold of my kin

The Bar Scene

The music buzzes
The drink fuzzes
The singer dances
The barmaid fences
The drunkard penses
On thoughts he had never
While sober thought over

Sinking to the Floor

Lay your head back on the floor
Drink the air in deeply
Hear the sounds
Then choose to ignore
The bustle, too demanding
Focus now upon yourself
Feel the world around you
Meld into cohesive health
I am one with the world too

A Beaut

"She's a beaut!" cried he
And set out to sea
On her, his beautiful sailboat
She had starboard and port
He fished off her sport
In the shade of her cansas canopy

She floated on waves
He sailed her for days
Across the closest ocean
Till he came upon
An island where on
He sought a new devotion

She sat alone
Tied to a stone
Awaiting his return
Till the hurricane came
And dragged her away
Her beauty left to burn

She #10

She is stronger than she looks.
She looks very pretty.
She picks the bar up off the hooks
And squats a hundred fifty

She is nice to everyone
Though she's not much for talking
She smiles and the whole world melts
Just because she's listening

She is making a career
Out of directing soldiers,
But soldiers working under her
May not respect her orders

It's hard to be a pretty girl
And hard to give advice
When those who should listen to you
Just think, 'She sure looks nice. '

Creativity Clots

You sent me a song?
Oh another one.
You keep sending soundbytes
So far I've listened notta one

I know it's how you like to
Communicate your thoughts
But listening all the way through
My own creativity clots

I know that it's important
To show you that I care.
My shirking what you want
Should make you aware

We are not where we once were
You are not my muse
When working, I don't see you there
Your texts, I just peruse

I've promised you so often
To never say goodbye
The words made hard can soften
Since I frequently deny

The truth is I don't need you
But I keep you hanging on
Cuz I dread someday I'll miss
After you're truly gone

So I scroll on my phone
And click a goddamned link
Please do not be daughtry
Please, song, do not stink

Then I listen to the song
You claim is in your head
To once again explain
The words you've never said.

Except, my love, you have said,
Time and time again.
Someday we will be both dead
And we'll have no words unspoken

Criticism

I send you a poem
Something I worked quite hard on
You say nice! Then send me
Another you "just thought" on

I say writing's hard
You say writing's easy
When distinguishing quality
I think your poem was lousy

I try my best
I compliment a point
I don't criticize the rest
But I don't your poem anoint.

Check Your Own Work First

I'm glad you're always learning
But that doesn't mean that I
Should lay by what I'm earning
As you invent a new knot tie.

Just because you're interested
In making something cool
Doesn't mean I'm invested
In what you make, as a rule.

It's not that I won't support you.
I want you to do well
But last graphics you drew
Made my cranium swell

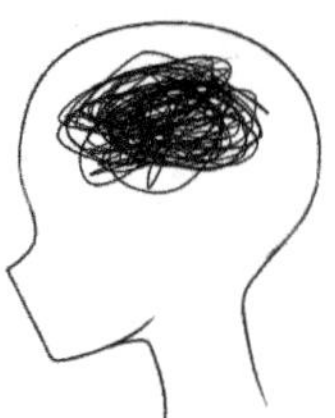

So don't give me a seizure
But don't give up on dreams
I just ask, if you're not sure
Double stitch those seams

Another Friend

I called you
I texted.
I messaged
sometimes too
My words went
unanswered.

'Crap,' I thought.
There goes another friend.

I agonized my choices
I worried what it meant
I regretted my voices
And thought I should repent

Then one day I call you
Somewhat from the blue
I hear your cheery tone
As if you never left me alone

Oh I did nothing wrong
You only switched your phone
You did enjoy my song
Though your response a stone

A Raven and His Human

Once there was a raven
Who flew beneath the clouds.
He searched up high
He searched down low
For friends that could be found

There too was a human
Who roamed away from crowds
He hiked up high
He dove down low
Deep inside the ground.

One day when he was walking,
For once along a street,
When he heard a loud "Hullo!"
But not a trace of feet

The human walked on further,
But not a soul he saw.
He thought perhaps he'd heard a ghost
Until he heard a caw

Looking up, the human,
Saw a big black bird.
Hullo! The pretty raven cried
And not another word.

I'm Sorry

I'm sorry.
I shouldn't have woken you up.
The words just made me think of you

I worry
When you're too weak to lift a cup
Do my words now cause pain, too?

Please hurry.
Your mind is so far away
I am right here, must you away stray?

I scurry
Down corridors in your mind
Hoping by looking I'll you remind
Of silly things.
Stupid things.
Shared in our brains.
Though I don't know what, of your side, remains

Ho dilly
Heigh ho.
Can we go back to then?
With me a fair maid and you a dragon?

I'm sorry
I shouldn't have woken you up.
I just missed you

Christalline

Your soul is something crystalline
That cannot be shaped nor sharpened
When other pieces broke and reformed
I saw your spirit hardened

Your body is a masterpiece
No sculptor could ever create
Each chunk of mortar chipped off
Was taken away by fate

Spontaneity and Fate

Spontaneity and fate
Went on a date
To find some things in common
They both valued time
And could both value wine,
The difference there was how often

Fate sat in a chair
And Spont said "Hey, look there"
Then swiped a peck on his cheekbone
He asked "What's the rush?"
But that same cheek did blush
Where spontaneity's lipstick shown

"We must at this hour,"
Said fate, his face dour,
"Review the options at hand.
We should now inspect
And carefully reflect..."
Spontaneity gave him a flower

Build in Me a Baby

Build in me a baby
Fold my flesh to fill
Hold you deep inside me
Careful not to spill

Make my womb a paradise
Make in me a home
With sugar, spice and all things nice
A fertile plot of loam

Latch onto me child
Who has yet to be
Someday you will grow wild
But now stay safe in me

Cuddles

I lay beside your body
And I don't want to move
The conforms of your pilates
Fit in all my grooves

I touch your warm skin
I feel your pulsing heartbeat
I give in to your sin
I feel our bodies exchange heat

There is no comfort greater
Than what I'm feeling here
The greatest worldweaver
Could not texture this sphere

This globe of curly brownish head
This supple luxuriant flesh
Laid across my lovers bed
To my love replenish

I love you I say with my eyes
I love you with my hands
The words itself you can surmise
From the way our figure stands

You. Oh lover of my life.
The one I'll love forever.
I'm so glad I became your wife
Whatever your endeavors

The Night Tree

Night has come upon me.
I lay beside my love
And visions of a world tree
Reach my brain above

The rustling of wind
The swaying of the leaves
The sturdy trunk, now dimmed
Reaches above the eaves.

This tree cannot be present
It's layered over the house
It does not rip through our rent
It does not wake my spouse

And yet I lay here staring
At this ethereal tree
Jutting from my bedroom.
Jutting from within me

The leaves have curled in darkness
But when approached by light
The unfurled leaves a starkness
The branches are invisible bright

So I close my eyelids
To join where my family sleeps
Awaiting dreams the tree bids
Creep into my evening peeps

When I wake in the morning
I know it won't be there
The night tree needs no warning
To simply disappear

www.ingramcontent.com/pod-product-compliance
Lightning Source LLC
LaVergne TN
LVHW051245200726
843510LV00011B/1702